Sacred
in the
Simple

Making Mantras Part
of Christian Living

Mary Lou Kownacki, OSB

With an Introduction
by Joan Chittister, OSB

LIGUORI
PUBLICATIONS

One Liguori Drive
Liguori, MO 63057-9999
(314) 464-2500

ISBN 0-89243-780-4
Copyright © 1995, Mary Lou Kownacki
Printed in the United States of America
First Edition

Cover design and interior art by Wendy Barnes

Special thanks to
Buddhist monk,
Thich Nhat Hanh,
whose *Earth Gardens*
invited these mantras.

Introduction

There are songs we sing in our hearts over and over again—school songs, love songs, and Christmas songs—that take us back year after year, day after day, through all the days of our lives. No matter how many times we hear them, no matter how many times we sing them, these songs bring back all the feelings, sights, smells, and memories that make them significant. That's why we sing them. They bind us to the past, they root us in the present, they give us a future we can trust. Mantras are the same kind of memory cues and emotional markers.

What Is a Mantra?

A mantra is a word, phrase, or prayer that is repeated over and over until it drives all other thoughts from our minds and roots us in an ideal that gives us meaning and direction: "Home, home, home," "Jesus, Jesus, Jesus," and "Holy, holy, holy," for example. Whatever word, phrase, or prayer we chose, it is meant to move us out of where we are and into a deeper space, purer air, perfect silence—the center of ourselves where lesser gods goad our thoughts and grip our minds in vain. A mantra opens the soul.

The purpose of a mantra is to put us in touch with something inside ourselves that no amount of distractions, no degree of noise, no whirl of activity, no type of intrusion, can ever dispel. A mantra restores us to that point of ourselves that has higher ideals than the daily demands on our hearts.

The Sacred in the Simple is a collection of contemporary mantras which, if we say them often enough, we might well become them. The world would surely smile on us if we became hospitality, reverence, gentleness, compassion, and praise. More than that, the world might become them with us.

Try it. Say these mantras over and over again until, one day, you realize that they've become a part of you. You find yourself being a loving listener, a gentler friend, a walking gloria through all the cacophony of life. "As you are, so is the world" Ramana Maharshi teaches. It is time to begin so that the whole world can become a softer place because of us.

JOAN D. CHITTISTER, OSB

On Awakening

The sun rises
again.
Is this not a miracle?
Opening my eyes wide
the glory of God
is revealed.

- Keep something beautiful where you can see it upon awakening.

- Breathe deeply; smell the air.

- Be mindful of God's presence around you.

- Protect the ozone. Don't use Styrofoam or aerosol sprays.

- Pick a flower. Remember that it was made for you.

On Washing

From ice and rainstorm,
the water flows over me.
Through bedrock and wellspring,
the water flows under me.
In the wide circle
of rivers,
the water flows
around me.
All living things
depend on water
flowing.

- Take a walk in the rain.

- Use water sparingly
  while brushing your teeth.

- Hand wash your clothes and dishes.

- Drink a glass of fresh water slowly.

- Be aware of the water you use. Pray for
  those who must walk for water each
  day.

On Opening
Scripture

If today I hear God's voice,
may I not resist
a softer,
more compassionate
heart.

∾ Spend time each day
   with the Scripture.

∾ Share with others or write in a journal
   how the Scripture has changed you.

∾ Choose a passage from the Scripture
   and repeat it during the day.

∾ Read the daily news
   from the perspective
   of the Scripture.

∾ Memorize a psalm.

On Dressing

What I learn from lilies
that grow in fields
is a gentle and simple spirit,
natural beauty,
and how to rest confidently
in God's arms.

∽ Try to wear and use
  natural fiber clothing.

∽ Foster a spirit of simplicity and beauty.

∽ Take a yearly inventory
  of your clothes and possessions
  and develop a habit
  of sharing your gifts with the poor.

On Eating

Oh, taste and see
in this morsel of bread
the faces and tears
of those who hunger.

- Enjoy a meal with friends.

- Experiment with occasional vegetarian meals.

- Cut down on the amount of meat you eat.

- Fast one day a week as a way to remember those who are poor and hungry.

- Join a group committed to ending world hunger.

- Volunteer at a food bank or soup kitchen. Take a long, loving look at the homeless and hungry.

On Walking

Tread softly.
A gentle step upon the earth
enables earthworms,
sweet potatoes,
and yellow flowers.

- Take a daily walk
  and enjoy God's beauty.

- Exercise regularly.

- The next time you go outdoors,
  spend a few minutes picking up litter.

- Use only biodegradable products.

- One day a week, use an alternative
  means of transportation: bus, subway,
  train, bicycle, walking.

- Go barefoot in the early morning dew.
  Feel the earth.

On Working

May my mind think no harm,
may my lips speak no harm,
may my hands do no harm.
May the children of tomorrow
bless the work I offer.

- Compliment a coworker.

- Share your talents and time
  with the community.

- Purchase an item handcrafted
  in a Third World country,
  and remember the person
  who made it.

- Pressure multinational corporations
  to pay just wages
  to Third World employees.

- Choose work that is life-giving
  and contributes to the well-being of
  others.

- Spend some leisure time with children.

At Midday

Let not the heat
of the noonday sun
wither my spirit
or lay waste my hopes.
May I be ever green,
a strong shoot of justice,
a steadfast tree of peace.

~ Think of a contemporary martyr.
  Pray for a virtue that you see
  in that person.

~ Renew your commitment
  to peace and nonviolence.

~ Work with others to bring about
  a more just and global society.

~ Promote the use of the world flag.

~ Live with integrity. Say yes
  when you mean yes;
  and no when you mean no.

On Community

Engrave this upon my heart:
"There isn't anyone
you couldn't love
once you've heard their story."

∾ Forgive a past offense—really forgive.

∾ Think of each person you meet today
as important. Try to bow inwardly
to that person.

∾ Make a yearly inventory
of the ways you serve
the community.

∾ Consciously avoid conversation
that is destructive of others.

∾ Make a point to be present
to others at meals.

On Stewardship

Everything on earth is filled
with sacred presence.
Let us bow down
and worship.

❧ Care for a plant or tend a garden.

❧ Support electoral candidates
   who run on an environmental platform.

❧ Use the earth's resources sparingly
   and with gratitude.

❧ Recycle whenever you can.

❧ Delight in a poem.

❧ Listen to a symphony.

On Hospitality

Open wide my arms
that the suffering of the world
may come in.

∾ Talk to someone about the meaning
  of world citizenship.

∾ Eliminate a personal prejudice.

∾ For one day, be conscious of how
  you use the words *us* and *them*.

∾ When a guest comes to your house,
  say, "Thanks be to God."

On Silence

Hush, tree toads in the swamp.
You screech as loudly
as the voices within me.

❧ Help create an atmosphere
   that fosters contemplation.

❧ Commit one day a month
   to silence and solitude.

❧ Take time today
   to bring yourself to peace.

❧ Enjoy a hearty laugh.

❧ Identify three things in yourself
   that you dislike. Befriend
   and redeem them.

❧ Speak from the heart—
   tell someone you care.

On Resting

One more day to serve.
One more hour to love.
One more minute to praise.
For this day I am grateful.
If I awaken to the morning sun,
I am grateful.

- Do not let the sun go down
  on your anger.

- Since we all came into the world
  with nothing, everything is a gift.
  Think about that.

- As you fall asleep,
  repeat a sacred word.

- Tonight look at the stars.
  Let the universe fill you with wonder.

- Visit a cemetery.
  Care for the grave of one you love.

- List your blessings.
  Follow your dreams.

About the Author

Sister Mary Lou Kownacki is a Benedictine nun. She is Executive Director of the Alliance for International Monasticism and the former National Coordinator of Pax Christi USA.